D1580071

ADORABLE
BUT DEADLY
CREATURES

by Charles C. Hofer

raintree
a Capstone company — publishers for children

Raintree is an imprint of Capstone Global Library Limited, a company incorporated in England and Wales having its registered office at 264 Banbury Road, Oxford, OX2 7DY – Registered company number: 6695582

www.raintree.co.uk
myorders@raintree.co.uk

Hardback edition © Capstone Global Library Limited 2022
Paperback edition © Capstone Global Library Limited 2023
The moral rights of the proprietor have been asserted.

Edited by Aaron Sautter
Designed by Heidi Thompson
Original illustrations © Capstone Global Library Limited 2022
Picture research by Kelly Garvin
Production by Tori Abraham
Originated by Capstone Global Library Ltd

978 1 3982 2259 5 (hardback)
978 1 3982 2258 8 (paperback)

British Library Cataloguing in Publication Data
A full catalogue record for this book is available from the British Library.

Acknowledgements
We would like to thank the following for permission to reproduce photographs: Alamy/Rick and Nora Bowers, 15; Shutterstock: bogdan ionescu, 17, FtLaud, 7, James Laurie, 23, Jeff W. Jarrett, 22, Jeremy LANGLET, 4, kaschibo, 9, Magalie St-Hilaire poulin, 21, Papzi555, 11, Pavel Kovaricek, 27, Sahara Frost, 13, StoneMonkeyswk, 5, Szasz-Fabian Jozsef, 1, 29, Thorsten Spoerlein, cover, 19, TRossJones, 25. Design elements: Shutterstock/Fer Gregory

Printed and bound in India

CONTENTS

Words in **bold** text are included in the glossary.

CUTE KILLERS

The world is full of deadly animals. But not all deadly animals are huge and scary. Some can be small. Some can be cute. And these killer cuties are found in **habitats** everywhere. They live in dark jungles. They wash up on beaches. They may even sleep in your back garden!

Cute but deadly animals come in all shapes and sizes. Some are big and furry. Others can be small and colourful. But they all have deadly features to help them survive in a dangerous world. Some creature features are used for defence against **predators**. Others are used to catch and eat **prey**.

So you've been warned.
These animals are cute – but deadly!

PUFFERFISH

The ocean is full of dangerous animals. It's home to sharks and killer whales. But not all deadly sea creatures are big predators.

The pufferfish is a perfect example. It looks harmless. But when threatened, it uses a great defensive trick. It gulps down a lot of water and expands its body. Sharp spines stick out from its skin. The pufferfish blows up like a spiky balloon to scare off predators.

The pufferfish's skin is also **poisonous**. The poison from one pufferfish can kill several adult humans. In some countries, pufferfish is a special food. But this deadly fish needs to be prepared carefully. Every year several people accidentally die from eating poisonous puffers.

FACT

Poisons are dangerous chemicals that some animals and plants can produce. They use poison as a defence to scare off threats.

FEATURE FILE

Common name: Pufferfish

Habitat: Coral reefs in shallow ocean waters

Range: Warm oceans around the world

Size: Can expand its size, length ranges from about 2.5 centimetres (1 inch) to more than 61 cm (2 feet) Weight up to 13.6 kilograms (30 pounds)

Deadly features: Poisonous skin and sharp spines

BLUE-RINGED OCTOPUS

If you see a cute little octopus with blue rings, don't touch it! This octopus is deadly!

The southern blue-ringed octopus is about as big as a golf ball. This pint-sized creature lives in shallow ocean waters near Australia. The blue-ringed octopus likes to live in rocky areas. The rocks help it to hide during the day. It comes out at night to hunt crabs and shrimp. The octopus uses its eight arms to catch and hold onto its prey. Its strong **suction pads** help to break open hard shells.

The octopus's mouth is near the centre of its body. It's pointed and sharp like a bird's beak. The deadly creature delivers powerful venom through its bite. It can **paralyse** prey, making them easier to eat.

FACT

Venom is another type of poison some animals can produce. Venom is used to capture or kill prey. It's usually delivered through a bite or sting.

FEATURE FILE

Common name: Southern blue-ringed octopus

Habitat: Shallow rocky reefs, coral reefs

Range: Coastal Australia

Size: Length 5 to 10 cm (2 to 4 inches)
Weight up to 28 grams (1 ounce)

Deadly features: Venomous bite, strong suction pads

FLAMBOYANT CUTTLEFISH

The cuttlefish's name makes it sound cute and cuddly. But beware. This creature is fearsome!

Cuttlefish are related to octopus and squid. Like them, cuttlefish are **nocturnal**. They are mostly active at night. Cuttlefish live near the ocean floor. There, they feed on small animals such as shrimp. Cuttlefish have special skin for defence. They flash bright colours when they feel threatened. This warns predators. It says, "Back off, I'm dangerous!"

The cuttlefish's skin isn't just flashy. It contains a powerful poison. If a predator bites it just once, it won't make the same mistake again.

TOXINS: MOTHER NATURE'S DEADLY BREW

Toxins are dangerous natural chemicals. They're found in both poison and venom. They can make people very ill or even kill them. Toxins can attack and destroy skin tissue or muscles.

FEATURE FILE

Common name: Flamboyant cuttlefish

Habitat: Coral reefs

Range: Indian Ocean, South Pacific Ocean

Size: Length 6 to 8 cm (2.4 to 3.1 inches)
Weight up to 400 g (14 ounces)

Deadly feature: Poisonous skin

BLUE DRAGON SEA SLUG

The blue dragon sea slug is a strange ocean animal. It looks a lot like a pretty bird. But don't be fooled. The colourful slug is a killer – and a thief!

Sea slugs are **molluscs**. They are closely related to snails and clams. But they don't have hard shells for protection. Instead, they have a better defensive trick.

The blue dragon sea slug's favourite food is the Portuguese man o' war. These creatures are related to jellyfish. They have poisonous cells that sting. When the blue dragon eats a man o' war, it steals these deadly stinging cells. The blue dragon stores them in its "fingers", which are called cerata. The stolen stingers make the blue dragon sea slug poisonous. Its sting can make a person very ill.

FACT

The Portuguese man o' war's stinging cells work like tiny poisonous harpoons.

FEATURE FILE

Common name: Blue dragon sea slug

Habitat: Shallow ocean waters

Range: Hawaii and other Pacific islands

Size: Length up to 3 cm (1.2 inches)
Weight up to 100 g (3.5 ounces)

Deadly feature: Poisonous stingers stolen from their prey

ARIZONA CORAL SNAKE

Many of the world's snakes have venom. These deadly snakes kill thousands of people each year.

But not every dangerous snake looks scary. The Arizona coral snake lives in the southwest United States and Mexico. It's very colourful. Its body has bright bands of yellow and red. These colours act as a warning to predators. They say, "Don't touch me!"

Arizona coral snakes have some of the world's most powerful venom. They are deadly hunters of lizards, frogs and smaller snakes. But don't worry. These snakes are very shy and rarely bite people. They spend most of their time hiding in rocky areas. They also have very small mouths and a weak bite.

FEATURE FILE

Common name: Arizona coral snake

Habitat: Desert mountain areas

Range: Southwest United States and Mexico

Size: Length 33 to 53 cm (13 to 21 inches)

Deadly feature: Powerful venom

FIRE SALAMANDER

Fire salamanders are found in forests in northern Europe and Asia. They mainly live under moist rocks and logs on the forest floor. There, these colourful killers feed on tasty worms, slugs and bugs.

Fire salamanders have bright yellow and orange markings. These colours warn predators to keep their distance. Why? The salamander's skin is very poisonous. Just one bite can make a predator extremely sick.

This crawling cutie has another deadly defence. Special **glands** behind its eyes store poison. When threatened, the salamander squirts this poison at an attacker. It aims for an enemy's sensitive eyes or mouth. What a deadly trick!

FEATURE FILE

Common name: Fire salamander

Habitat: Evergreen forests

Range: Northern Europe and Asia

Size: Length 15 to 30 cm (6 to 12 inches)
Weight about 20 g (0.7 ounce)

Deadly features: Squirting poison and poisonous skin

GOLDEN DART FROG

The golden dart frog lives in South American rainforests. It's cute. It's tiny. And it's one of the world's deadliest animals.

Golden dart frogs can be yellow, orange or green. These bright colours are a clear warning to predators to stay away. These little frogs have very poisonous skin. Just one tiny frog could kill 10 adult humans!

Golden dart frogs eat ants, flies and other small insects. Scientists believe their poisonous punch comes from their diet. Toxins in their prey are absorbed by the frog. The toxins build up in the golden dart frog's colourful skin.

FACT

Some native people use the frog's poisons to hunt. Hunters scrape the poison off the frog's skin. They then put it on the tips of their darts and arrows.

FEATURE FILE

Common name: Golden dart frog

Habitat: Rainforests

Range: Colombia, South America

Size: Length about 2.5 cm (1 inch)
Weight about 28 g (1 ounce)

Deadly feature: Poisonous skin

RACCOON

With cute masks and fluffy fur, raccoons are adorable animals. They're so cute they could almost be pets. But beware. Raccoons can be dangerous. They are often found in cities and towns. They are drawn to food and rubbish we throw away. This sometimes causes trouble between people and raccoons.

Like other animals, raccoons can attack when they feel threatened. They don't want to attack – they're just scared. Some raccoons can carry **rabies**. This deadly disease is caused by a **virus** that attacks the brain. Unfortunately, there is no cure. Raccoons can give humans rabies through a bite. That's why it's important to give these wild animals plenty of space.

FEATURE FILE

Common name: Raccoon

Habitat: Forests, cities and towns

Range: Most of North America and Central America

Size: Length up to 91 cm (36 inches) with tail
Weight up to 26 kg (60 pounds)

Deadly feature: Spreads disease

MONARCH BUTTERFLY

Monarch butterflies have dazzling orange and black wings. But these pretty colours have a purpose. They act as a warning to predators. The monarch butterfly is very poisonous to many animals.

Monarch butterflies get their poison from their food. Monarch caterpillars live on milkweed plants. These plants are found across much of North America. The caterpillars eat the tasty milkweed leaves. The leaves contain a powerful toxin. It turns into a strong poison in adult monarch butterflies. This poison acts as a defence against hungry predators such as birds.

LOOKALIKES

Other butterflies imitate the monarch's look. Queen butterflies look very similar to monarchs. Their wings also have bright orange and black patterns. But the queen butterfly is totally harmless. This imitation game is called **mimicry**.

FEATURE FILE

Common name: Monarch butterfly

Habitat: Grasslands and prairies

Range: Southern Canada to Northern Mexico

Size: Wingspan 10.2 cm (4 inches)

Deadly feature: Poisonous

KOALA

Big-eared teddy bears? Not quite. Koalas look adorable. But people should keep their distance. These cute and cuddly furballs can be dangerous.

Koalas are **marsupials**. This type of mammal has a pouch to carry its young. Koalas live in forests in Australia. They stay hidden high in the treetops. Koalas are mainly active at night. They can sleep for up to 20 hours each day.

Koalas often look sleepy and slow. But they can be aggressive. They often fight over **territory** or food. Koalas are also very protective of their young. They have sharp teeth and large claws. They won't hesitate to attack when their young are threatened.

FACT

Koalas are often mistaken for a type of bear. But koalas are not related to bears at all.

FEATURE FILE

Common name: Koala

Habitat: Forests

Range: Eastern Australia

Size: Length up to 84 cm (33 inches)
Weight up to 14 kg (31 pounds)

Deadly features: Sharp claws and teeth; aggressive when threatened

HONEY BADGER

The honey badger is closely related to the skunk. Unlike skunks, they're not very smelly. However, the honey badger can be quite dangerous. It has long claws, sharp teeth and a fierce attitude.

Honey badgers eat just about anything. Birds, rabbits, snakes and insects are all on the menu. The honey badger gets its name because it likes to eat honey. These creatures seem to have no fear. They'll climb right into a buzzing hive full of angry bees to steal tasty honey.

Honey badgers are famous for being mean. This is what makes them so dangerous. Like most animals, a honey badger will attack if it feels it's in danger. The honey badger will also attack much larger animals than itself – even humans.

FEATURE FILE

Common name: Honey badger

Habitat: Forests, deserts, mountains

Range: Africa, Middle East, Asia

Size: Length up to 76 cm (30 inches)
Weight up to 14 kg (30 pounds)

Deadly features: Sharp teeth, wicked claws, ferocious nature

WHITE-FOOTED MOUSE

What's furry, adorable – and deadly? It's the white-footed mouse. These mice are some of the most common **rodents** in North America.

The white-footed mouse is known to carry deadly diseases such as hantavirus. This virus can cause high fevers, headaches, difficulty breathing and kidney failure. The deadly virus is found in the droppings of the white-footed mouse.

These cute, yet dangerous, mice like to live near humans. They might live in the basement or loft of a house. In these dark places, mouse droppings can build up. When cleaned up, the virus can mix with dust and float into the air. If people breathe in the virus they can get very ill or even die. As adorable as these creatures are, they can be incredibly deadly!

FEATURE FILE

Common name: White-footed mouse

Habitat: Forests and grasslands, buildings

Range: Throughout most of the United States

Size: Length about 18 cm (7 inches) with tail
Weight about 28 g (1 ounce)

Deadly feature: Spreads disease

GLOSSARY

gland organ in the body that makes and releases natural chemicals

habitat natural place and conditions in which an animal or plant lives

marsupial type of mammal that carries its young in a pouch

mimicry way of copying the appearance or actions of an animal or plant for defence against predators

nocturnal active at night and resting during the day

paralyse cause a loss of the ability to move or control the muscles

predator animal that hunts other animals for food

prey animal that is hunted and eaten by another animal

rabies deadly disease that people and animals get from the bite of an infected animal

rodent mammal with long front teeth used for gnawing; rats, mice and squirrels are rodents

suction pad body part used by an animal to hold onto objects

territory area of land that an animal grazes or hunts for food

toxin poisonous substance produced by a living thing

virus germ that infects living things and causes diseases

FIND OUT MORE

BOOKS

Adaptation and Survival (Life Science Stories),
Louise and Richard Spilsbury (Raintree, 2016)

Cutest Animals on the Planet, Jennifer Szymanski
(National Geographic Kids, 2021)

Octopuses (Animal Abilities), Anna Claybourne (Raintree, 2013)

Reptiles (Animal Classification), Angela Royston (Raintree, 2015)

WEBSITES

www.bbc.co.uk/cbbc/shows/deadly-60
Track down 60 of the world's deadliest animals!

www.dkfindout.com/uk/animals-and-nature
Find out more about animals and nature.

INDEX